Like a weaver long trained in his craft, Jeff Gundy blends many strands into nearly every poem, with precise variations of color. He's particularly adept at drawing out the nuanced grays of daily life—as when he notes how a line of cardboard boxes set out on the curb last night "sag in the rain like the saddest, smallest, oldest mountains ever"—till one begins to look everywhere for those little touches of *presence*, in his poems and in the world beyond our own windows. But then there are the reds and oranges, the places where he teaches us to *play* with what we know: "It seems only reasonable to sense / that we live in a country full of ghosts," or, as he walks a path in a "Rainy Sunday in Ravenna": "The trickle becomes a creek almost, / it murmurs its creek-words for any soul that passes."

Between those two poles (the concrete and the fanciful) the poet constructs his meditations on everything from the red shed in his dying neighbor's yard and on into the nature of determinism, Lorca's duende, or his own years growing up in Midwestern America. Jeff Gundy *observes*, with a humble, winsome eye…and an ear for song. He says, "When / I pause, look up, around, something begins / to swirl and echo." What a joy it is to follow the trails he traces across the page—and out into the world. Finishing this book, my impulse (as with all favorite books of poems) is to return to the beginning and start it all over again!

—Terry Hermsen, author of *A House for Last Year's Summer*

Other Books by Jeff Gundy

Poetry Collections:
- *Abandoned Homeland*. Bottom Dog Press, 2015.
- *Somewhere Near Defiance*. Anhinga Press, 2014.
- *Spoken among the Trees*. Univ. of Akron Press, 2007.
- *Deerflies*. WordTech Editions, 2004.
- *Rhapsody with Dark Matter*. Bottom Dog Press, 2000.
- *Flatlands*. Cleveland State Univ. Poetry Center, 1995.
- *Inquiries*. Bottom Dog Press, 1992.

Poetry Chapbooks:
- *Greatest Hits 1986-2003*. Pudding House Publications, 2003.
- *Surrendering to the Real Things*. Pikestaff Press, 1986.
- *Johnny America Takes on Mother Nature*. Pinchpenny Press, 1975.
- *Back Home in Babylon*. Pinchpenny Press, 1974.

Essays/Creative Nonfiction:
- *Songs from an Empty Cage: Poetry, Mystery, Anabaptism, and Peace*. Cascadia Press, 2013.
- *Walker in the Fog: On Mennonite Writing*. Cascadia Press, 2005.
- *Scattering Point: The World in a Mennonite Eye*. SUNY Press, 2003.
- *A Community of Memory: My Days with George and Clara*. Univ. of Illinois Press, 1996.

Bottom Dog Press

Huron, Ohio

WITHOUT A PLEA

POEMS

JEFF GUNDY

HARMONY POETRY SERIES
BOTTOM DOG PRESS
HURON, OHIO

Copyright © 2019 by Bottom Dog Press
All rights reserved.
This book, or parts thereof, may not be reproduced in any form without permission from the publisher; exceptions are made for brief excerpts used in published reviews.
ISBN: 978-1-947504-13-4
Bottom Dog Press, Inc.
PO Box 425, Huron, OH 44839
Lsmithdog@aol.com
http://smithdocs.net

CREDITS:
General Editor: Larry Smith
Cover & Layout Design: Susanna Sharp-Schwacke
Cover Art by Merrill Krabill

ACKNOWLEDGEMENTS:

As always, I owe thanks to too many people to name for the life that brought these poems into being, but I must first thank Bluffton University for ongoing support, and my wife Marlyce for continuing to put up with me. Special thanks, also, to Keith Ratzlaff and Clint McCown for late-night intensive hotel room workshops, Terry Hermsen and Jean Janzen for years of advice and inspiration, and Julia Spicher Kasdorf for stalwart friendship and necessary feedback on an earlier draft of this manuscript. The Quarry Hollow writing group (Susan Carpenter, Mary Grimm, Susan Grimm, Mary Norris, Tricia Springstubb, Donna Jarrell, Laura Walter, Charles Oberndorf, Jackie Cummins, and Lynn Powell) has been a great source of companionship, critique, and literate and/or raucous conversation. And though I don't suppose they will read this, I am grateful to all the creatures and things of this earth for allowing us all to live here, so far.

The memory of my friend, neighbor, and sometime collaborator Gregg Luginbuhl runs through and under many of these poems. Rest well, Gregg.

Many thanks to the editors of the journals and anthologies where these poems first appeared, some in different versions:

About Place: "Carefully Selected Quotations with Minimal Commentary"
Bloodstone Review: "That What We Love Exists in Time, Not Space"
Brevity: "Mud and Gravel"
Cape Rock: "Meditation on Gravel and Guilt," "Life in the Complex," "Gundy Puzzles Over His Failure to Change His Name or Take Off to New York City to Become a Songwriter"
Cincinnati Review: "Plain Advice"

ACKNOWLEDGEMENTS CONTINUED ON PAGE 93

Contents

Plain Advice 9

I. *Don't fight when you're hungry*
Late Summer with Mink, Duende, and Calamities of Varying Degree 13
"Nothing is Level There" 14
Things I Plan to Create Upon Achieving Sufficient Focus 15
Mud and Gravel 16
Why I Got Nothing Done this Summer 18
Privilege 19
Further Inquiries into Duende 21
Magpie on Highway 221 22
Carefully Selected Quotations with Minimal Commentary 24
The Listener at the Conference on Peacebuilding, or Playing the Spider 25
Theodicy with Tents and Masonry 27
Another Song 28

II. *A gap in the fence*
Speaking Truth in the Most Human Way 31
Cold Day in the Provinces 32
God Is Not Right, He Is Big 33
Rainy Saturday in Ravenna 34
Red Shed 35
Contemplation with Red Bridge and Windy Sunshine 37
Elegy in Two Places and Two Parts 38
That What We Love Exists in Time, Not Space 40
The God of Dirt 41
Where I Was Instead 42
Meditation on Solitude and Simplicity 43
September: 9 Variations 44
Late Spring in Old River Town with Guesswork and Bombay Sapphire Gin ... 46

III. *How empty, how full*
Determinism on a Summer Morning in the Midwest 49
Uneasy Fantasia from Quarry Hollow 52
Friday the 13th with Borges and Old Quarry 53
Notes toward Intuitive Geography 55
Zen & Blacktop 56
Traces 57
Meditation with Salal and Otters 59
Think Like a Tree 60
Meditation with Creatures and Late Sun 62

On the Way to Denver 63
Saturday with Crow, Fury, and Speedboat 64
Spring Ode with Robins and Mallards 66
"You Never End with Hello" 67

IV. *The boy who listened too hard*
Late Explanation 71
Meditation with Gravel and Quilt 72
Puff 73
Gundy Puzzles Over His Failure to Change His Name or Take Off to New York City
 to Become a Songwriter 74
The Scale Model 75
The Professor Undertakes Metaphor 76
Soft Tissue 77
On the Condition of Rural America 78
The Smaller Mysteries on a Winter Sunday Morning 79
Ponies 81
Some Sentences for a Man Who Won't Read Them 83
Nice People 85
Tablets 86
Life in the Complex 87
How We Learned to Love Our Bodies 88
Lessons of a Gentle Childhood 89

About the Author 91
Acknowledgements Continued 93

Ah, what an age it is
When to speak of trees is almost a crime
For it is a kind of silence about injustice!
And he who walks calmly across the street,
Is he not out of reach of his friends
In trouble?
—Bertolt Brecht, "To Posterity," trans. H. R. Hays

The soul knows for certain only that it is hungry. The important thing is that it announces its hunger by crying. . . . The danger is not lest the soul should doubt whether there is any bread, but lest, by a lie, it should persuade itself that it is not hungry.
—Simone Weil, *Waiting for God*

PLAIN ADVICE

Don't be foolish. No, be foolish.
Each of these trees was once a seed.

Look down the road till it's all mist and fumes:
of course your journey is impossible.

It's stupidly hot for September and yet here's
an eddy, a gust, something to stir you

as the high leaves of the walnut are stirred,
as fine droplets touch you, touch the table

and the deck, no explanation, no design.
And beauty is like God, mystery

in plain sight, silent, hesitating
in leaves and the shadows of leaves,

in the carved fish painted and nailed
to the railing, in skeins of cloud

and searching fly and pale blue
scrim of sky and seas of emptiness

and dazzle, fusion and spin,
fire and oblivion and all that lies

on the other side of oblivion.

I.

Don't fight when you're hungry

Late Summer with Mink, Duende, and Calamities of Varying Degree

> *Seeking the duende, there is neither map nor discipline. We only know it burns the blood like powdered glass . . .*
> —Federico Garcia Lorca, "Theory and Play of the Duende"

Sometimes there's a dead cicada on the driveway
near the back door, iridescent, almost weightless,
and that's only the beginning.

If you want the *duende*, sometimes you have to stamp your feet.
Sometimes you just have to look around, wildly or not.

Someday you'll look at the bulk pack of batteries and then just buy two,
so your children won't have to deal with the leftovers.

I think mink must be lonesome, sometimes, and hungry most of the time.

Don't fight when you're hungry. Don't drink when you're angry.
Don't dig into the chips until your wife goes to bed.

To speak of trees is almost a crime, said Brecht, *when there is so much injustice.*
He was right, but *almost* is the important word.

Sometimes the wild, silky part of yourself can't resist
sneaking into the henhouse and killing all the pullets.

The editor said Marianne Moore lied, that she didn't hate poetry,
but what did he know?

It's not the worst thing to admit that you hate what you love most.

The word *sometimes* belongs somewhere in that sentence.

My friend Ray says he needs finer wire mesh around his henhouse.
The mink was slender enough to sneak in.
The pullets were six weeks old, too big to drag out.

The mink killed seventy, one after another,
but couldn't take a single one off to feast on.

The hogs ate well that week.

"Nothing Is Level There"

—Bob Dylan, on Duluth

Consider the world as an evil tree. Hans Denck did, in 1560.
"It has never borne as much evil fruit as in our day,"

he wrote. "But there is not that much to bewail us yet.
There is more, by far, to be thankful for." The gray skies

of Duluth, yes, and the mysterious foghorns, and the slanting
streets. Or the joys of living far from the big lake and its

merciless howl, in the flat corner of a state that is nowhere
so crooked, where the creeks can barely decide which way

to run, where the swells and dips of the mother's soft body
are enormous and arcane as the sky, where winter trees

twist into the pale clouds. So it is necessary to be grateful.
And to see the world clearly. And to dream of the great change

but avoid the error of the Israelites, the golden calf that
Moses burned and ground to powder and forced them

to drink. What am I drinking, I wonder some days, when
the coffee has an edge that seems new and unsavory,

uncanny even. Will this carry me off, end my years of ease
and comfort, cast me into the long spiral? Not so far from here

the Russians are bombing hospitals. Not so long ago
we bombed a hospital. The explanations were plentiful

but not convincing. *The world is an evil tree* works as well
as any. "Truthfulness is crucial," wrote C. D. Wright,

recently deceased, in a book I read closely but had almost
forgotten. "The tree has never borne so much evil fruit,"

said Hans Denck in 1560. And still there is not that much
to bewail us. Still we shall be thankful for the crooked streets,

for the broad waters, for the deep and irregular earth.

Things I Plan to Create Upon Achieving Sufficient Focus

> *I have to focus so hard I seem to create it.*
> —Dean Young, "Rothko's Yellow"

Small things first—a pixie, maybe a bridge troll.
Sweatpants dressy enough to wear every day.

Sport coats comfortable as sweatpants.
An endless supply of balmy spring days to be

warehoused nearby, available on demand.
Some days of steady, warm rain, likewise.

A set of bells that will subtly rearrange hearts
and minds, nudge the fearful fist open, unfurrow

the fretful brow. A place of generous exile—
on a mainly habitable moon of Saturn, say—

for those unwilling to heed the bells. A transport
mechanism, foolproof, safe, and allowing only

photos of baby goats and moving tales
of adversity overcome to return. A salve

for all wounds, a syrup for all coughs, a balm
for all fevers. A touch to ease heartache,

to bring release to the captives, bread and
warmth and roses to the poor, open hearts

and eyes to the oblivious rich. A dust to heal
the waters, make the plastics vanish,

cool the oceans, mend the sky. And lunch.

Mud and Gravel

1.
Gravel and mud, mud mixed with gravel, gravel sinking gray and jagged into the soft brown mud as the spring storms beat down and pass by, as puddles fill and ebb away, as the heavy yellow diggers and draggers and loaders prowl in their loud slow way. This sloppy wide mess that runs down one side of the creek, across the sidewalk and the street and back the other side of the creek will be for the good of all—so we are told and mainly believe. The storm waters and the foul waters should not mingle.

The mess is temporary, we believe, the costs manageable. The mud and gravel and slimy tracks and branches broken, trees uprooted and undermined, all these are small and temporary against the greater good, against keeping our sour and difficult wastes sealed off from the innocent rain.

So we pick our way, try to ease our minds. This is not the Somme after all. Any day now the green pipes and the concrete junctions will be laid and joined and covered, the mud leveled and smoothed. The new grass will be sowed and sprouted, the sidewalks patched, saplings planted where the lost trees stood.

We have seen the old photos, the bare fields that are wooded now, the fresh streets, the first rough buildings. We close our eyes and can almost remember those days and the days before, the days of no streets and no village, only the deep woods and wetlands, traces the deer follow to the water, to the clearings where they browse at dusk and dawn, their faces lifting solemnly at what might have been the whisper of a stealthy paw, of a moccasin.

2.
A hundred years ago my country entered the Great War. This morning the radio told of horses and mules shipped over the ocean to drag machines and food and men through the mud, the splatter, the broken bits of trees and men, flowers and guns.

In 1914 the entire British Army owned 80 motor vehicles. Between 1914 and 1917 the U. S. shipped 1000 horses a day to Europe, many of them half-tamed animals from the Great Plains.

The horses were so valuable that the Germans plotted to infiltrate the docks at Newport News, to infect the horses with anthrax and glanders.

The plot failed, but 8 million horses died in the war, plus countless mules and donkeys—better suited for conditions on the front, but like the horses, large and attractive targets. Very few were volunteers.

3.
No man or animal was suited for the mud of Flanders, the mud of Passchendaele, the mud that was a slime of dirt and shit and piss and blood, iron and casings and shrapnel and flesh in all stages of disintegration.

The mud was *sucking* wrote Siegfried Sassoon, wrote Herbert Read, wrote Richard Aldington, wrote Wilfred Owen. It entered through the mouth, the eyes, the skin. Men sank in to their knees, and deeper. Men foundered and despaired. One was trapped for 65 hours before being rescued.

Hell is not fire, hell is mud, wrote someone in a trench newspaper.

Tolkien, at the Somme with the Fusiliers, caught trench fever and was sent home. Much later he had Sam Gamgee come face to face with dead things, dead faces, in the stinking mire of the Dead Marshes.

4.
My room is quiet this morning. The machines are still as stones, the wind tugs at the Douglas fir and the bald cypress near my window. The mud runs along the creek, this side and the other, like the scars of surgery on the largest animal anywhere.

To get here I walked around the yellow tape, the orange pylons, over the raked gravel waiting between the wooden forms.

I have seen, we have seen, the earth heal and change. Flanders is lovely again. Things grow from the mud. New greens erupt irresistible as gravity, as rain, as love.

Every mess is not a crisis. Eggs must be broken. Today is not tomorrow, or yesterday. Everything is connected, and every thing is precisely itself.

5.
Like the mud and the gravel, the creek and the trees, like you and everyone you love and despise, I am spinning through space and time on a course too fast and wild for any sober reckoning.

I have a good bed, and no rifle. The wars are a long way from here. My shoes are only a little muddy.

Why I Got Nothing Done this Summer

> *Nothing gets done without committees. This is a fact of modern life. . . . it's also frequently true that committees get nothing done.*
> —Stephanie Krehbiel, "The Perception of the Problem"

I didn't go to a committee meeting all summer.
Probably this explains it all.
I'm getting left off the best committees, and have been for ages.
The "Let's have a Crusade!" committee.
The *Walden* committee.
Etc.

Instead of getting something done,
I sat on the glider on my screen porch,
noticed that it needed varnish. I didn't paint it,
but I did later paint the porch floor,
prodded by my wife who also hates committees
but likes paint. And the porch ceiling.
And the steps down to the basement,
which were spectacularly neglected.
Other parts of the house could use paint,
but there are limits.

At school I'm known for sulking through meetings,
while some of my worthy comrades love them so much
they prolong them to spectacular lengths.
Sometimes I leave my body entirely,
voyage to other worlds actual and imaginary,
and return to find the group still wandering
through fields of earnest redundancy.

Still, even the dullest meeting must end at last.
We are thanked and released, like cows after milking.
Yet even then my comrades linger and converse
while I flee with unseemly haste
into the rain or the December darkness.
Minutes arrive the next day, the next week,
but the hours do not reappear.

Privilege

Some people I know save dryer lint, and make crafty objects with it.

Some earnestly beseech me of a Sunday morning to reflect upon my privilege and take action.

Some make friends with every stranger in range, invite them home for dinner, while I smile vaguely and hang back, slip out the door and home, sink into the loveseat.

I do reflect on my privilege, daily.

I'm getting old but the house is paid off, and my wife still puts up with me as much as I deserve.

I have been pondering the purchase of a thousand-dollar bicycle to replace my five-hundred-dollar bicycle.

The people I love have mostly not been shot by strangers, starved in camps, or hounded from their homes by deranged fanatics.

It's true, some have bellies full of cancer, bad backs, pains chronic and acute.

Some are differently abled, as we say these days.

My church leaves its doors open day and night, for ideological and idealistic reasons.

A year ago we placed security cameras at the doors, for other reasons.

My college friend Dwight is living alone in the house his parents built, still working at the same bad job, wondering what he'd do if he retired.

He Skyped me today as he almost never does, said *fixing the roof cost me three months' pay*, said *I took a day's vacation and almost went crazy*.

The connection was bad and both of us lost half of the other one's words.

One of his brothers is in Vegas, the other in Dresden.

The only other people he mentioned were his shrink and his boss.

The first costs too much and the second doesn't pay him enough.

~19

On my $500 bike I can ride faster than most people think is useful or necessary, and farther too.

I think sometimes I have too many friends to do any of them justice.

When my wife leaves town half of my mind is guilty-happy for the time alone.

I wander the house, eat vast crude saucepan meals, let whim and duty wrestle out each hour.

I don't call up anybody to have lunch.

Are you retired yet, Dwight asked, as everybody does.

Closer than I used to be, I say.

He still has his hair, not even gray, but his eyes looked weary, and he kept telling me that his computer needed a new power supply.

A few minutes in we lost each other entirely. I tried to call back three times before his power supply supplied enough power to fire up his old computer one more time—who still has a Gateway?—and we talked another twenty minutes.

I spent a month's salary on a new roof, Dwight told me.

I said *I guess I should let you go* to Dwight but I meant *I'm worn out by the bad connection, worn out wondering what to ask or to say*.

The house was quiet. I went down to the quarry, listened to the geese and catbirds, read the names of the veterans on the sign near the street.

A yellow leaf fell at my side. A fish surfaced and sank.

Further Inquiries into Duende

> *Never pretend to be a unicorn by sticking a plunger on your head.*
> —Martín Espada
> *It is not a question of aptitude, but of style. . . . Tired of lies and circles,*
> *Descartes fled along the canals to listen to the singing of drunken sailors.*
> —Federico Garcia Lorca

In Juneau we walked the boardwalk along the surging stream,
both banks lined with prettified former whore houses.

A bald eagle perched on a post, severe and indifferent.

I wouldn't dare tell the scruffiest bald eagle it lacked *duende*.

My students have many opinions about *duende*,
though we failed to come up with a concise definition.

Does *Phantom of the Opera* have *duende*? R.: Yes. C.: No.

Can you achieve *duende* through feedback and distortion? Me: No. R.: Maybe.

Bach more than Brahms. But not all Bach, either.

Marley's "I Shot the Sheriff." Clapton's, well . . . But "Layla," both electric and acoustic.

Beyoncé, but not Britney.

Prince, that solo on "While My Guitar Gently Weeps."

Keats *and* Yeats. And Blake, almost too much.

Walt and Emily, both. Dark chocolate vs. a huge potluck with lots of desserts and baked beans and potato salad that maybe has been sitting out too long.

The Stones and the Beatles. But really, John more than Mick.

Soybeans, no. Wheat, no. Corn, in a bumper year.

The Rockies, sure. The Smokies, here and there.

In the prairies, only the sky.

Magpie on Highway 221

In the middle of my journey I turned off the interstate because my phone said I could save 14 minutes and the highway was busy and boring. What the hell.

Immediately it seemed a blunder—Highway 221 was narrow and twisty, dark woods on all sides, a ponderous truck with a burgundy-colored tank on its bed clogging my lane.

I was pondering which fracking-related fluids it might be hauling and how long I'd have to follow when the driver took a side road with a sign pointing to Site 53.

Then there was Prosperity, a string of houses on both sides of the road, some well-kept, many needing paint and labor.

I cruised through with my windows up and the AC whirring, the little car sipping at the fuel in the tank, carrying me along alone and nearly happy, on my way to see my poet-friends and explore in depth and detail our anger and despair at the atrocities of late capitalism.

Birds flew low across the road as though on crucial errands, and four orange cones marked where the blacktop had collapsed into the ravine.

Most of the road was still good, most of the trucks going the other way. At a crossroads a driver who could have pulled in front waited for me to pass.

Many signs cautioned about trucks entering, many signs offered the best prices for oil and gas rights and numbers to call.

I had no rights to sell so I kept driving, following every curve and dip. Almost no one was out.

The hills were green and lush. There were more houses beyond Prosperity, squeezed into narrow gaps and flats near the road.

One of the birds I swear was a magpie, a western bird though small colonies escaped from the Pittsburgh zoo were reported as late as 1969. It was not a kingfisher, not a killdeer, not a woodpecker either pileated or red-bellied. It could have been a hairy woodpecker, though the guide says these are uncommon. It could have been an eastern kingbird, though its markings seemed bolder and stronger, all magpie. I've seen them in Colorado meadows, in mountains, never so far east.

I only glimpsed the bird as I sped on, as it sliced across the road and out of sight.

Twenty miles more, swerving and slowing for hills and curves, making bad time, thinking that I was falling behind, that I'd be late, that I'd miss the party.

A birder in Mahoning County saw two magpies in 2005, published pictures and an article in *The Ohio Cardinal*.

When I found the main road I was still on time. Later I looked at the big map, and found I'd driven twenty two-lane miles instead of forty on the freeway.

If I lived just past Prosperity, if the plant had closed and I had sold my gas rights for the money to paint the siding and the eaves, to patch the foundation and have enough for a case of Iron City now and then, would I sit on the narrow porch and watch the trucks roar by six times an hour? Would I believe my eyes if I saw a magpie slip across the road and into the trees?

Carefully Selected Quotations with Minimal Commentary

But we will learn, she insisted. There are delights, impediments,
and chairs. Who *are* we? Von Ranke would laugh when he discovered

a false narrative. How was your academic pedigree formed?
What do you mean, love the Lord with your mind? Power

& hierarchy & all those isms, really big solar panels, identity silos,
third way thinking: a circle? a rectangle? The cradle-to-prison

pipeline? Trust, compassion, stability. Hope? Guilt? Even soldiers
spend most of their time not killing each other. I ask students

to write reviews of the bad books we're reading instead
of the brilliant one I am entirely sure I will write, someday.

As we seek the Light let us not forget the unreasonable efficacy
of mathematics, issues of emergence and reductionism,

echoes and glints of the multiverse. In my negative remaining
minutes, please imagine that I spoke of God in nature,

eloquently and at some length. But next, the task of reconsidering
our beliefs, the problems of leaving stuff out and of a certain

self-righteous subjectivity. Yet God has time, and so we also
have time. Let us resist the notion that we are autonomous entities.

Could it be, that the world once was aflame with fate? A hundred
thousand killed as witches, and yet we still have no reliable studies

of levitation or the flying friar Joseph. We must be tender as we
approach these sources. *Nie wieder Krieg.* Down with competition,

up with synergy. Don't be boring. Don't be bigoted. Be absolutely
dogmatic. God asks: *How will you name the world?*

The Listener at the Conference on Peacebuilding, or Playing the Spider

> *Till the bridge you will need be form'd, till the ductile anchor hold,*
> *Till the gossamer thread you fling catch somewhere, O my soul.*
> —Walt Whitman, "A Noiseless Patient Spider"

1.
According to the people from Dakar, Bogatá, Kolkata, etc., my town in the Ohio fields may not be the center of the world.

One asks, *I traveled for forty-one hours to speak for fifteen minutes?* So we listen hard for fifteen minutes.

Flinging threads into the void seems so 19th century. And yet, to catch hold somewhere . . .

2.
Would you rather be a button, a hook, or an eye?

In the end, the eye sees too much. The ear cannot close. The body cannot refuse to be touched.

When the bad daughter escapes, what does she do with the rest of her life?

Someone said: *it is easier to love the deprived in far corners of earth than our own inconvenient children.*

Your failure may open a window to the soul.

If we can tell the stories simply, without explanation . . .

The man who survived the concentration camp watched *Hogan's Heroes* with his granddaughter, years later, both of them laughing.

A groundhog dwells under the rocky ledge just outside the apartment door.

3.
The oppressive community is itself complicated, but the shunned find this small comfort.

Wind moves. Sand whispers.

Sometimes there may be no clear, efficacious, nonviolent solution.

~25

I will only ask God to forgive them, said Miriam.

Who will be the conscientious objectors in the wars against women, against the poor, against the planet?

4.
Sometimes the silence of mourning is all we can offer.

Can we eroticize peace?

Everything is connected, but not even the wind harp can say exactly how.

To build soil from dust and ashes.

To argue with God and the world as it is.

To notice the groundhog, and let it be.

Theodicy with Tents and Masonry

1.
When my unemployed faith reappeared as boredom,
it seemed a diplomatic triumph. But just about then

animals began to intercept me in my wanderings.
I grew more and more open to their solicitations.

Trees are probably fearless, but the forest should have
known better than to show off like that. We had long known

that God pitches his tent among the castoffs at the base
of the mountain, and that fair Dawn, with her fingertips

of rose, is another living power. Staring, said X, is good
for what passes as the soul. When we crawled from

the tunnel, the square was strewn with masonry.
The cathedral's back was ripped open, as if bleeding

from a terrible wound. And then the hand of a child.

2.
Asked for whom she wrote, Y replied *Myself and strangers*.
Time makes its witnesses forget. But the trees

should have known better. John Henry and Staggerlee
once belonged to us all. The animals began

to intercept me and the others, cast off at the base
of the mountain. Even the humble word *brush* gives off

a scrap of light. Some sensations have lost their fascination
for me, but not all. Fearless or not, the witnesses

keep talking. Dawn seems a diplomatic triumph.
God pitches his tent in the body's hidden glen.

Another Song

> *I went out to the hazel wood,*
> *Because a fire was in my head . . .*
> —W. B. Yeats, "The Song of Wandering Aengus"

I went down to Riley Creek
because my heart was sore and sad,
and I slipped twice and laughed and swore
and scared a muskrat from his bed.

I threw some rocks into the creek,
and a bat flew in the groping dusk
where a yellow backhoe crouched and slept,
dreaming of broken stone and mud.

And leaves of yellow and of brown
lay like scraps of a tattered book
torn to pieces by a girl
who only sought an easy song,

some danger, joy and misery,
some heartache, a sweet and liquid kiss
in a greeny field. What else to do,
why not, the land scoured bleak,

cold rain denting the black earth,
too late, too far, the borders closed,
the towers of Paradise aflame
and cooled already, ash and smoke.

II.

A gap in the fence

Speaking Truth in the Most Human Way

One can use the words of religion, she noted,
while specifically not meaning them, at least

not in the old way. T____ was a devout Mormon
for a decade, but then he came out. Language

is a residue anyway, and yet the world is full
of little possibilities for love, like those little

Reese's cups, like those wafers of chocolate
almost too bitter to savor. Might we live

as belated witnesses, bearers of shards
not entirely our own, glimmers glimpsed

through late leaves, over dry fields where
the slave bodies once labored, where

slave sweat soaked deep between rows
of cotton? How can we put the eroded,

loaded world back into language?
Life changes the absolute history of time,

claimed the Chinese historian. *Watching
a thing, we wish to inhabit it,* said the writer.

We wish to consume it, said the predator.
Faith must trample under foot all reason,

sense, and understanding, said Luther.
It seems only reasonable to sense

that we live in a country full of ghosts,
some still too devastated by grief and trauma

to speak in any human language, some
clamoring to be heard, shining on the vine,

drying in the drought, drowning in the flood.

Cold Day in the Provinces

>—for Sarah Nahar
>"*I have hardened my heart only a little.*"
>—Robinson Jeffers

The zipper of my down coat snagged for the umpteenth time.

Somehow the fabric never tears.

Three sets of tracks beaten in between the classrooms and Old Ropp.

The former governor says her son's PTSD is the president's fault.

Now that I'm looking, I hear the chittering of birds everywhere.

Tree broken twenty feet up, a crooked upside-down V, snow brilliant on the slanting trunk.

A spokesperson describes recent acts by a foreign government as a) "a blatant and unacceptable breach of the most fundamental tenets of civilized behavior," and b) not a surprise.

Icicles dangle from the bumpers of the students' cars.

Another governor says he'll pray for the kids with their blood full of lead, that he feels terrible, that it wasn't his fault.

A sparrow perches on the No Parking sign.

"Creative maladjustment" is the phrase of the week.

The sycamore, snow in its high branches, a revelation in white and gray and three more grays.

God Is Not Right, He Is Big

The news isn't all bad. July and August
were the hottest months in human history,

but a family found the pet tortoise
that went missing in 1982. The low cloud

above me passes under the high clouds
like a souped-up Civic passing on the right.

I've been all over this island and still
have no names for most of the trees.

Despite the urgings of good people
I do not find Job comforting: all that

swag and bluster, mean and useless
as Oz before Toto pulls the curtain.

The plenitude and manifold texture
of things, this comforts me a little.

My old friend is in a hospice bed,
his beard gray and wispy.

His blond granddaughters, both born
months early, are up too soon,

happily demanding love and cereal.
The low cloud is nearly past,

the high clouds are scattered and lit
by the early sun. Not everyone is safe.

Not everyone is warm. "God is not big,
he is right," that wise fool William Stafford

had the dandelions say, but they were
already drying up, forgetting

everything, loosing their frothy seeds
to scatter and settle as they might.

Rainy Saturday in Ravenna

The leaves are not a carpet, but then what are they?
Two crows fly over, calling.
The wind is not a voice.
The crows are not messengers.
The path is exactly the path.
The woods go deeper than I thought they would.

Trickle of water, old Jeep tracks, older deadfalls.
Box of clay targets by the launcher: "Fragile as eggs."
In the mud it's best to walk beside the path, not on it.

Was there a spring I didn't see?
The trickle becomes a creek almost,
it murmurs its creek-words for any soul that passes.
Anyone can drink, or dip a finger, or step over,
or follow to where someone built a little shelter of sticks
big enough to hold a child
though not safe from the rain.

Among all the live trees, the snags where the owls,
bats, and woodpeckers make their home.
And a few green ferns among the leaves.
And the lazy curves the water has discovered on its way.
And the way seams open along the frozen creek.

There are probably enough poems in the world.
There are not enough leaves, not yet.

And when I turn back, chilled and hungry,
when I wonder is this right, how lovely
that what I half-remember and what lies
around the next turn are the same.

Red Shed

Gregg put up the storage shed along the property line years ago, and built the chain link fence later, when he and Karen got their first dog Norman, who loved to roam and annoy the neighbors. The shed had the mower, garden tools, the usual assortment of stuff mostly left there to rust or rot. It was cheap, not quite flimsy but hardly a brick shithouse, and the years were not kind. A nail worked loose on the side facing us, then more, and one windy day a swath of red metal siding was banging and shaking as I went past on my way to school, banging harder when I came home.

By then Gregg was barely getting outside, maybe to sit on the deck for an hour. His studio downstairs stayed dark, the wheel empty and still, half-made cups and plates drying slowly. I'd pass by the shed and see how bad it had gotten, the stuff inside awkwardly exposed, and think that I should just bring over some screws and a driver and get things back in place as best I could. But I was always in a hurry. I offered once, vaguely, and Gregg and Karen smiled and said thanks, but they had a plan.

His son-in-law did tear down the shed, one weekend while I was away. They put the mower in the garage after a few days, found places for the other tools and damp, half-empty bags of potting soil and fertilizer.

The last time Gregg and Karen came for dinner with our little group it took all three of the other guys to ease him out to the car. We walked across the back yard while Karen drove around the block, helped Gregg out of the car and up the porch steps. His muscles felt like soup under the skin. Still he spoke calmly, thanked us as we got him to the big chair with the power assist. I walked home with the feel of his arm, so strong and capable not so long ago, tingling in my fingers.

Everybody with a house knows how things want to fall apart, to collapse, to leak. Today I climbed out the back window onto the roof, put some more tar and a piece of aluminum on the peak where the garage roof meets the addition. It only leaks when it rains. I've been up there eight times, used up six tubes of roofing tar, still can't figure out where it's getting in. Maybe this time, I keep saying.

The downstairs toilet leaks too, not on the floor but somehow through the joint between the tank and the bottom part. I've tightened those bolts six times, fearful of breaking the porcelain, and still we hear the swoosh as it refills every ten or fifteen minutes. Not a fast leak, and we can pay the bills. But it drives me nuts. Today I put a wrench on the nut underneath, a big screwdriver on the slot inside, and cranked it down some more. It didn't break. I haven't heard it filling since, but the radio is on.

Gregg and Karen's second dog, Harold, lived for years after he went blind and feeble, achy with arthritis. Once he took off after a squirrel and ran straight into one of the old fire hydrants Gregg collected. He was gentle in his old age, not especially friendly but charming in his decrepit way. Sometimes they spelled his name Herald, and I liked that even better.

Gregg's ashes rest in an urn he shaped with his own hands. The thousand beautiful things he made of clay and glaze remain. Some mornings I drink coffee from mugs he formed and glazed and fired. The ceramic fish he made just for me, with my poem carefully inscribed along its belly, hangs on the wall, his hands almost touching it still.

There's a gap in the fence where the shed used to be.

Contemplation with Red Bridge and Windy Sunshine

The space between two people never quite closes. That's
all right. It's the rub of surfaces we need anyway, the slow

brush of hand on arm, the quick hug as we discover
an old friend has gone gray, that he's reading on a hard

chair in the back room, leaving most of the house to strangers.
It's all right to leave him there, maybe, to walk across

the red bridge and into the woods, travel the worn paths
in windy sunshine. Turning left each time will bring

you back. It's all right, maybe, to explain that you won't
be back till late, that you hope for coffee in the morning,

for a small table upstairs to spread out your books and papers,
most of which you won't open before you pack up to leave.

The space between two people can open like a net, collapse,
dangle loose and empty, ready to catch and hold, to bind.

Elegy in Two Places and Two Parts

> *And sometimes, even music cannot substitute for tears.*
> —Paul Simon

1.   Quarry Hollow, Kelleys Island

Word is, the owners were only here twice this summer.
I had to pull the door out from behind the bed and

lean it up in the frame. At least they ripped out the old,
disgusting carpet, and the new floor's still pretty clean.

For once we made the 6:00 ferry, though I forgot
the fresh mozzarella I was supposed to sprinkle

on the casserole. Gregg is still in the hospice bed,
his uneven breathing all that's left. Today a student

read her poem about her artist roommate's crafty pen
and I remembered Gregg turning clay on the wheel,

talking as his hands centered and shaped it, graceful
and efficient as a hawk carving circles in the air.

It's muggy, the window ledge is full of mold, the foldout
bed is mushy and dingy, the wine glasses are plastic.

There was a dead mouse in the upstairs toilet.
And I'm feeling like the guy who fell from the silo

and lived, like the Christmas spruce nobody picked
before it got too big for anyone's living room.

2.   Maple Grove Cemetery

We parked in the wet grass, found the little urn
his father made. It was propped on a box

next to Gregg's parents' stone, out in a far corner.
A scrim of trees, the browning fields beyond.

The family was late, as they always are—
We were just talking and forgot the time, Karen said.

There were a few white chairs, some scripture,
some words from the interim pastor, a decent guy

with a trim beard who barely knows any of us.
It's not his fault. I read the poem I'd brought,

and we sang two verses of "Amazing Grace."
After the prayer someone nodded and pointed

through the trees, and when I shifted I saw
what I hadn't seen, two full-sized white-tails

and two half-grown, all of them watching us
with that enigmatic earnest look deer have.

Do quiet beings always seem wise to noisy ones?
We considered each other for a little while.

Then Karen and the children got up, bent one by one
to touch the urn, and we followed them away.

And I thought: the deer knew we would be here,
they came in hope that we might join them,

step through the thin line of trees,
cross the field into that other life.

That What We Love Exists in Time, not Space

> *If we're not supposed to dance,*
> *Why all this music?*
> —Gregory Orr

The sunflower's yellow gaze is not anxious.
It does not whisper or fret as it wheels

to meet the sun. It sails the time stream
like the monochrome branches outside my window.

They sift the January fog without complaint,
 as if the winter will never end.

The guitar rests in the upstairs room,
not thinking of me. In two hours

I'll be finished with meetings and papers,
done with explaining and judging.

I will pile the homely and awkward words
with my own, make a heap on the desk.

I'll douse the light, and close the door.
At home I'll climb the steps and open the case,

pull the pick free, check the strings,
let my hands take the places they know.

We'll pick up the song, slowly at first,
vanish into the sweet tangle of sound.

What do they matter? I have no answer.
I don't care. Whatever becomes of me,

no matter how fast those notes fade,
they will have been, strung between

me and the guitar, afloat in the room.

The God of Dirt

came up to me & scowled
& asked me what we'd done
with the treasure. Sorry,
I said, I can't even
tell you where it went,
Lake Erie, the St. Lawrence,
we barely noticed.

Well then, said the god
of dirt, *taste & see*
& there she was,
unknown & yet
I knew her,
had seen her
in some hollow of the mind,
flitting & calling,
& not for me,
not to me.

Listen said the god
of dirt & she sang
liquid & lovely
tangled up my body
& mind in blue
and gold and green
thickets of song.

Then she whispered
something soft to me
& spun herself away,
whispered to me
something soft
that I will not say.

Where I Was Instead

> *Late have I loved you, beauty . . . You were in fact inside me,
> but I was not inside you.*
> —St. Augustine, *The Confessions*

I was forgetting to register, forgetting to order books,
forgetting to turn off the lights on my way to bed.

I was still somewhere on the Pennsylvania Turnpike,
stuck among four semis in a snow squall, barreling

down a mountain curve at 77 miles an hour, the little car
skittering with each gust. I was waking up every hour

to blow my nose and pee, navigating interior caverns
dripping with yellow snot. I was eating too many chips,

checking scores on my phone, flicking through photos
of people I didn't know. I was reading the laments

of young mothers worn down by the second baby, the job,
the house, the first kid still in diapers. I was avoiding

the real, bitter news, the trickling glaciers, the manifold
miseries, the grinning orange nemesis, just for today.

I was listening to Caleb my firstborn grandson explain
how he drove the giant tractor right out on the road,

how he saw the Arch so big you can see it from everywhere.
I was watching Owen laugh and pick up berries with

the salad tongs, eat them one by one, sing as he forked
in pieces of pancake, come thou fount of every blessing,

banging the table, laughing, tune my heart, he's not yet two
and yet he has the tune down flat, also some of the words

and all necessary expression, I laughed and sang and beat
time with him, oh, come thou fount, oh tune my heart.

Meditation on Solitude and Simplicity

Pay here says the sign but I walk on by,
the street is filled with people and nobody

is paying. Men are assaulting the pavement
just outside Jamba Juice but I trust it will

be well in the end. My table is near the restrooms
which are occupied. The guy with the broom

has a beautiful purple shirt. The girl waiting
is biting her lip. She goes to the door

and hesitates. I think about being smart
vs. being useful. My pen is nearly dry

but I have another. It takes a lot of people
to provide this much solitude. Alfred

North Whitehead urges us to seek simplicity,
but not to trust it. Would I trade my life

for any of these others? No, no, yes, maybe.
Only if it came with a didgeridoo. Only if

it came with a name tag. Only if rides
on the free mall tram were included.

Only with blonde curls and almost
too young to be my daughter. Only

if I could have mine back any time.

September: 9 Variations

1.
What's left to say? Here I am, dismal and dissatisfied for no good reason, prowling old notebooks, ready to plagiarize myself or anybody. Yesterday I boasted of my skill at breaking down cardboard boxes, at knocking things down, sending them off and believing them gone.

2.
Don't lose hope, Jeffrey, says the message from the former president.

3.
The beauty of windmills, an awkward and pragmatic beauty, like the heron's or the stork's. Years in the making, expensive and complicated, engineered and calculated, requiring access roads and giant cranes, buried cables and many tons of concrete poured and then hidden. They seem lonesome even in their togetherness, blades thrumming their monotonous notes, cupping the invisible wind, sifting for power, changing one energy into another.

4.
All this while I'm waiting for B. who's seven minutes late, who asked me to read her summer chapters which are full of typos, dull description, and tedious adjectives. What will I tell her anyway? What harm will another humdrum, self-published novel do to the world?

5.
All this in the prison of privilege, one modestly tedious day after another. Every day I hear of a new poem, a new book, by somebody diverse in one of six or seven ways that I am not. I read some of these, and love some of them. What's left to say?

6.
This spring for once I put the cages on the tomatoes right when I planted them. The next day I found three of them bent, twisted, scattered, and when I told M. she remembered some young guy walking through the back yard the night before, he must have stumbled into them in the dusk, got mad enough to fling them around. I found one in the snow peas and two others crumpled as if it were their fault for being in his way through my garden in our backyard when he passed through on his way God knows where, drunk or high or love-blind or full of hormones and conviction, did he scratch a hand, a knee, bruise a shin, swear, commit the unpardonable sin, tell his beloved when he reached her at last?

7.
The world is smarter than we are, my friend Erin told the students. No, she said the *work* is smarter than we are. It must be true, though I've spent my life thinking I'm smarter than most people. Yet I've also known I lack the greed and meanness of the truly great, the magnitude I mean, not the qualities themselves. My emotions, like my trials, are petty and minor and Midwestern. So be it.

8.
But then. I could have a swollen testicle and have to skip the big bike ride on Sunday. I could have five adjunct sections of freshman comp at three different schools. I could be trying to convince myself to stay with a guy who's beating me up, or leave a guy who's beating me up. I could have to walk three miles for water. I could live in a country ruled by a mean, bitter, ignorant, self-absorbed would-be tyrant.

9.
B. showed up just before lunchtime, apologetic. She went to work out and just forgot, can we still meet, when. We toss some times around. She's busy. I hate giving up my lunch hour, but we agree, lunch on Monday. She tells me then that she wrote the terrible first chapter, the pages of tedious and adjective-soggy description, three years ago. She knew it was lame but couldn't bring herself to edit it, she forgot to tell me, she was embarrassed. The pools of pink liquid still have to go. The boy can't be homeless and living in a shack at the same time. Still, the girl and her sister are both pretty good, the underground cavern, the village full of crystals. And the windy mayor, we agree, must disappear, but the snails on the windowsills have to stay.

Late Spring in Old River Town
with Guesswork and Bombay Sapphire Gin

The poet reads a poem called "Snow," full of metaphor
and light. Behind him is a big old window and behind that

a tree, its leaves twisted just out of shape by the uneven
old float glass. Not metaphor but things, I guess, not things

but the way things are seen and pressed into language
like keys into wax. The poet's arms are behind his back.

Maybe God woke up, he says. I may be remembering wrong,
confusing distance with death. The stars are a night

full of guesses. The leaves do exactly what they do,
and so does the window. Only to the watcher is it strange.

Only in Madison, Indiana, a river town that used to be
something. There was the broad Ohio, the Michigan road,

the riverboats and the factories and then the railroad,
before the other railroad came, and then all the other roads

that passed it by. People still find mussel shells with round holes
where buttons were drilled from them. Now the riverboat

restaurant won't open till two on Saturday. *Too much rain
this morning*, said the waitress, *the cook is still working on the fryers.*

We can come back, but won't. In the Filling Station
liquor store the clerk said she loves the Bombay Sapphire

I brought to the counter, but can't afford to drink it.
I knew that for three drinks in the hotel bar I could get

the whole bottle, so I just smiled, and she smiled back,
and I walked back to our room on the second floor

of the Riverboat Inn. My wife and I poured our glasses full,
then went to sit on the balcony, the two of us alone

with the quiet night, the distant river. And the darkness
eased into town, and then, as if God had awakened, the storm.

III.

How empty, how full

DETERMINISM ON A SUMMER MORNING IN THE MIDWEST

1.
There's no such thing as free will and that's bad, or so says
Stephen Cave in *The Atlantic*. I guess that explains my decision

to read his whole grim article this morning, when I had plans
to walk around town, mail a package, buy a retirement card

for Susan, have a cup of coffee uptown as I always think
I should but rarely do. The problem, says Cave, isn't that

we don't *have* free will but that we need to think we do.
"It seems that when people stop believing they are free agents,

they stop seeing themselves as blameworthy for their actions."

2.
Dostoyevsky said, *If God is dead, everything is permitted*,
but the claim has not been proven to my satisfaction.

There are tulips and a daffodil on the table, in a glass
mostly full of water. There's a child's orange coat hanging

by the door. Who can say when the gates will open,
or what they'll reveal? Lisa's five or six tables away,

but her voice is the only one I can hear. Not the words,
just the tone. She passed along what sounds like bad news,

though not a catastrophe. What am I doing here?
Anywhere? It feels like I'm free, but only because

I have no idea what to do next. OK, I have several
ideas, just none that seem halfway interesting.

Out on the sidewalk a woman with a child's hand
clutched in hers passed one way, then back the other.

3.
Blonde on Blonde is fifty years old. Dylan is still touring.
There are songs that mean more to me than most

of the Bible. I have fair-sized chunks of the Bible
and dozens of Dylan songs "by heart," which means

"lodged in my brain, to emerge at unpredictable moments."
Should I leave them by your gate? Should I wait?

4.
I have to go pee or just go home. There's nobody at home,
nobody in my office, I'd be safe either place, it would

seem like I could do anything I wanted. Maybe not
disappear, or fly, or grow hair on the top of my head.

I could get in the car and drive straight north to the lake,
or cross the bridge to Canada, or take the small roads

across the open prairies till they dwindle into traces.

5.
MS Word fixes some of my typos, but not all of them.
People I know keep wandering along the sidewalk.

The woman I thought was Susie isn't. The sky
is gray but no rain yet. The spring has been miserable.

I pay young folks to mow, spread mulch, things I could do
but just don't want to. I get on the bike and tear around

the country roads instead, come home sweaty and pleased
with myself. The tomatoes are still in their little plastic pots.

The broccoli is leggy and sulking. Who wants to believe
it's all my fault? Who wants to believe it isn't?

6.
"Wherever you go, you take yourself with you,"
says Neil Gaiman, also "You can't make me love you."

I'm pretty sure that when he said *you* he didn't mean me.

7.
For years I've loved the notion of being lost,
thanks to Rebecca Solnit's *Field Guide to Getting Lost*,

not to mention Jesus and Thoreau. I've lived for decades
in the same house on the same street in the same town

but I've never quite gotten my head around being saved.
In an old poem I wrote something like "He decided to save

his soul, the way some people save / handkerchief boxes . . ."

8.
"Sleep," says Picard-as-Locutus. "He's exhausted,"
says Dr. Crusher. But he's telling them how to destroy

the Borg vessel before they assimilate everybody.
There are many ways to awaken. Some are fatal.

Others will save you, if you can be saved, whatever
it means to be saved. Data figures it out quickly

and the cube ship explodes, leaving the Federation
safe and the members of the Borg collective

in a spectacularly less structured condition.

9.
I still don't know how to be myself and belong
to something at the same time, much less rest easy

where I am, however pleasant, however graced.
These days all I want to do is sleep, and eat,

and ride my bike for hours on the sweaty blacktops,
drain my water in the first ten miles, fog my glasses,

not bother to glance at the corn to this side,
the soybeans to the other, slow as little as I dare

at the blind corners where a pickup may be
blazing my way with its oblivious tons of doom.

Uneasy Fantasia from Quarry Hollow

In the back yard a mound of jumbled stone, overrun
with weeds and creepers, maybe an old barn, a wall,

a fortress, trees grown up in it, a lesson in texture
and limestone, gravity and the inscrutable past

and the space it allows for speculations of all sorts,
tedious, whimsical, brutal, just as the uneven planks

of the new picnic table invite complaints on the slovenly
craftsmanship of people these days. All of which

may interest only a man like me, cooling from my bike ride
on a sunny September day on this island, or The Island

as I nearly wrote before tripping over guilty recognition
of the many layers of my privilege. The Pope is in

New York, urging attention to the poor and the melting
of Greenland. My wife didn't pick up and is probably

out buying groceries. Both daughters-in-law are pregnant,
though we're not supposed to tell yet. I rode

every road on the island and some of them twice,
sweaty and happy, passed three golf carts and many

slow couples, all of us moving, some of us young.
There's music and laughter, wind in the trees,

there's no time and all time, crows, sparrows, chimes
and confessions. A moment in the giddy whirl

of the world. Moss on the stones. Sun on the moss.

Friday the 13th with Borges and Old Quarry

1.
> *To some futures, not to all . . .*
> —Borges, "The Garden of Forking Paths"

Words for the quarry: Broken. Scraped. Abandoned.
Why should I pretend this isn't miserable?

And yet the little trees offer their bold red berries
like a gift to whom it may concern. Many paths

lace the quarry floor, chunks of rock and meager firs
threaded among them, all the way to the lake,

the strange green shallow horseshoe lake where the boys
yell and leap in to impress their uneasy girlfriends,

where most of them surface with another shout,
and in most of the worlds I smile and wander on.

2.
> *Still another conjecture declares that the Company is omnipotent,*
> *but that it exerts its influence only in the most minute matters.*
> —Borges, "The Babylon Lottery"

My little path joins a bigger path but I bear off, stay close
to the rim. Limestone shattered into chips and shards,

shelves diving below like petrified swimmers. Late frogs sing
in the shallow pools. Beyond, a desert of rubble and scab.

And did God say, "That's good" here, too? A crow complains
from the brush, and a turkey vulture tips its wings.

On the lake shore geese gather in their grouchy flocks,
and cormorants arrow low and dark, each one alone.

3.
> *The insatiable search for a soul through the subtle reflections*
> *which this soul has left in others.*
> —Borges, "The Approach to al-Mu'tasim"

Last night I slept poorly on the dreadful hide-a-bed.
I woke every hour it seemed, no reason, then again

for good when S. started thumping cupboard doors
in search of coffee filters. The coffee was fine and strong,

and I told her no, she didn't wake me. Friday the 13th,
day of bad luck, day of killers and screams, but all that

is back in the other world. The quarry is quiet as Mars
or the moon and it seems necessary to attend

to every minor tree and trace and rock, every silence
and stir. The grasses have gone brown and thin

with autumn. The chipping sparrow and the crows
proclaim and complain, and tiny seed-heads shake

in the subtle, local breeze. The butterfly and grasshopper
are suddenly similar when they fly.

Notes toward Intuitive Geography

In my Ohio town the houses thin out fast
but there is always one more. Weather-beaten,

it waits in the cold like a feral cat
crouching under the bird feeder.

Pickups big as elephants roar
between vast stretches of shattered cornstalks
and the churned, puzzled soil.

The parking lots lie bare as the hearts of old men.

The streetlights make everything
seem softer and less empty than it is.

Limestone slabs of the creek bed
gleam like tusks in the moonlight.

And the roads run narrow and black all four ways,
pass the farm lots and empty churches
without stopping once.

Zen & Blacktop

If your name was Tom, you'd know what to name your cabin.

The bicycle breeze: a blessing, whatever the humidity.

Hum of the tires, buzz of the blacktop.

What sound does the wheel make when it's done turning?

What does the mindful biker notice? Wind, road, distance, speed, direction, traffic, weather, landscape, the mirror, breath . . .

The island has only ten roads, even counting the dead ends, and still I miss turns.

The mindful biker steers around the potholes, and sees the potholes coming, or so I do believe.

The little island runway tees with the road. The signs say *stay out, stop, look, caution*. Vehicles over ten feet tall are supposed to detour onto the other road, a mile west. The whole place seems deserted, but somebody must mow the grass.

Someday I'll say *fuck it* and ride headlong down the whole thing, just to do it.

Mindful is letting my monkey mind sway and glide and turn with the pedals, float and glow with the broad water as I swoop by, lean a little with the moored sailboats offshore.

How lovely still is the countenance of this earth, how earthy the sweat of my brow and my aging but strangely sturdy body as I slip and slice onward and lean to the easy curves and pass among the summer houses shut up already and the beach chairs waiting impeccably to be used or forgotten and the last slide of the island down to the wet seam where the land hesitates and then continues on its slow and obedient way.

Traces

> *That man standing there, who is he?*
> *His path lost in the thicket . . .*
> —James Wright, "Three Stanzas from Goethe"

1.
Mottle of snow all through the woods, rabbit prints
soon to vanish, saplings grown up between old tire tracks.

This way, that way? Scotch pine and sycamore.
In the hummocky, waterlogged meadow a slouched

black dog . . . dead? No, plastic. A real black dog
sniffs for traces, a hundred yards away. A line

of orange flags along the tree line, as if we couldn't
tell where the trees are, and a thin yellow wire.

The black dog and a white dog start to bark,
not at me. I'm almost disappointed.

2.
On such a day, in a January thaw, how to walk
is one problem, how to read this world another.

What to notice, to record, to imagine. There are paths
and tracks, some full of icy water. Open spaces

between the trees. A few brown leaves quiver
when all else is still. Long ago I read the claim

that our souls are *larger* than our bodies, and when
I pause, look up, around, something begins

to swirl and echo. It does not end at my skin.

3.
James Wright was drunk and mostly miserable
when he wrote his best poems.

Correlation is not causation.
Thank God for that.

4.
How to be smart enough to write a simple poem?
How much does the snow matter? The plastic bucket,

the rotted steel drum, the rusty wheelbarrow in the weeds?
The desire to turn for home. The desire to see more.

5.
The forty-foot fallen tree makes a very long bench.
Just beyond, the creek whispers over a lost limb.

All the branches break someday, Jim,
but they'll outlast both of us.

You knew that. It's all in the moments
we find, the moments we're given.

Last summer a one-legged jay hung around
our redbud tree for months, splashing

in the birdbath, sneaking up to the feeders
as though I might shoot him through the window.

Here, now, what spills from a culvert
made an ice sculpture like organ pipes,

like muscles rippling. Tomorrow
it will be water, and both of us gone.

Meditation with Salal and Otters

Today Baker's drifted even higher into the sky, the dark gap
grown a distance impossible to measure but clear enough

from far away. Closer, my measure-rock is underwater entirely
and the drift-log nods easily in a gap that was dry an hour ago.

Sharon's attacked the salal, cleared it back from the old log
so we can sit with our wine and discuss the great themes,

happy and half-drunk. The sky, the bay, the islands are a study
in shades of blue, pearly iridescence gathering over it all

as the last light hesitates in the trees. Suddenly cooler,
a gaggle of geese on the water, kelp, a clutch of river otters

bobbing and weaving. Twelve miles across to the mainland,
the mountains vague as promises, so much water between

and every day the ferries and freighters churn across it,
any number of beings dip and drink and dazzle themselves,

creatures grand and gentle, armored and furred, scaled
and skinned, empty and open. The drift-log slides east,

veering off from shore through no will of its own.
How many otters can live in all this water? At least four,

say my distant friends, and that's all that worries them.
The school of silvery fish think four otters is plenty.

But now four more slip down the shoreline, dark heads
only above the shimmery surface, heading east as the sun

sinks behind. And the mist is an aching golden pinkish
purple, an otherworldly wrap, a loose scrim to keep secret

what must be secret until the evening can be laid away.

Think Like a Tree

   —for Todd Wynward

Most of us are domesticated as cats, would be helpless as kittens outside the warm wombs of our houses.

Let's roar. Let's run away.

Fleeing Christendom never killed anybody.

OK, not many.

OK, not lately.

The prom king gave up his tuxedo and cummerbund, landed in the church where people with no papers were sleeping on the floor.

He painted his face red like Montezuma, carried a huge heart slung around his neck.

He grew real horns.

He made the revolution happen and washed the dishes too.

There are ways of living without kings, without walls.

Carrying all your own water will teach you things.

Sagebrush and the horse: two invasive imports that proved useful.

It's fine to live on the edge of the feral, to have neighbors who aren't human.

We can only save what we love.

We all have neighbors that aren't human.

Maybe the horns weren't real.

Still.

We can only love what we know.

We can never know enough.

That's no excuse.

Meditation with Creatures and Late Sun

A soft, suburban Surrey evening.
Two girls and a boy on bikes ride

back and forth through the ditch,
and a puppy who'd love to make friends

gets dragged away by his man.
So many lovely spaces on this earth,

so many creatures together and apart,
orca pods in the Strait of Georgia

with whale boats on every side.
Bill said he listened on the hydrophones

and heard newborns calling for their mothers,
the whole hidden tribe clicking and singing,

the thrum and drum of diesels and propellers
droning over, almost drowning them all.

The sun glows on the eastern mountains,
spills over us all like a father's judgment,

like the gaze of a mother who loves
her crazy children but cannot save them.

On the Way to Denver

From above, the clouds are always white. Color
is a construct. Words are bricks & mortar, studs
& drywall. Methane is invisible to the human eye.

Even this little bit of Nebraska, which may be Kansas,
is more than I can take in, cloud-covered or not,
the neat plots of fields & roads, wheat already green,

woods along the rivers still blurred & gray.
The arrow of an airstrip pointed northwest. The key
to shalom is dismantling: racism, patriarchy,

oligarchy, capitalism, and the use of vast abstractions
as markers of the so-called real world. From above
the clouds are pale and pure as a vast range

of my mother's mashed potatoes. And now
they are rising to meet us, we will learn how thin
they are, how empty, how full. They will hold

us up, they will let us down, the wheels will shriek
& bite into the irrevocable tarmac, the harsh
& fine & gritty surface of our days.

Saturday with Crow, Fury, Speedboat

—for Liz

1.
The universe is vast, but you're here, in this little corner of the world.

First station: weathered picnic table, the mouth of Scheele Preserve,
a sapling bent by a heavy vine into an arch, like the entrance

to no place special, or to no place, special. The obligatory, arrogant crow,
the compulsory mower. I'm a little warm from walking. Small tree

by the path, four wounds where it lost its best branches,
a few leaves too high for the deer. If the sign that reads

"no trespassing" is upside down, the top bolt rusted through
or vandalized, does it signal distress, or stress, or invitation?

2.
Rules are useful when the boundaries are lost, she said.

Don't swim after lunch.
Don't spit in the soup, unless it's obligatory.
Don't talk to strangers until you're old,
       and then don't talk at all.
Greet everything that moves,
including the squirrels.
You never know.
You never know.

3.
I never wrote the poems I have in my heart, and I might never write them.

She ought to be furious, my poet friend wrote long ago
about our other friend, who raised four kids before

she started writing poems. At the time I was mainly
not angry, so I didn't understand. Now on the beach

I know why the dog is leaping and barking furiously
at the end of the lake, I know how it feels to see

the terrible dark boats, to smell the dark men,
to watch as they turn the terrible weapons our way.

4.
    If everything is nothing, then I want to know this everything that's nothing.

The dog and the yelling children, the mother and father
enigmatic as shadows, all gone. The boat—just some

fishermen—on out of sight. Three miles out, a freighter
so vast I thought it was an island. And a bright orange

speedboat full of sound and fury: power means no need
to hide, means speed, means a shaking of the air.

And the shore and the waves continue to meet where
the boats dare not come, like old men who pass

each other daily and find no reason to speak.

Note: Lines in italics are from *For Isabel: A Mandala* by Antonio Tabucci, translated by Elizabeth Harris

Spring Ode with Robins and Mallards

My common town looks so different when I wander it
with a curious stranger, telling the usual stories, how we took

the beer money to put in the grand stained-glass windows.
The sky so blue that one could believe in forgiveness,

that our blunders and our grand ambitions will all be forgiven.
So much wasted time, yet the world seems almost intact.

Even the empty chairs are exactly where they should be.
The yellow sign is not the sun. But we get plenty of sun.

The neighbors can talk all morning and we'll talk right back,
we don't claim to be great but we are pretty good,

humble too but not in the dark Puritan way, more like
the common unlovely robins than the worms they live on,

the robins that lay their powder-blue eggs and let the shells
fall where they may, the prettiest parts of their lives, tossed

after a week or two. The days scroll past, dusky-rose evenings
glaring at the TV, red dawns groaned into the pillow,

sleeping off the latest mistakes. It would be easier without
the fear. But where do we put that down to rest, whose pockets

are big enough to hide it? It's true that worry never saved
anybody, but sunny optimism only works for Rudy, and

every time he says *Never better!* he's closer to a bruising.
Sure, the bald cypress is beating the odds again, sure

the mallards are shiny and plump with lust and spring,
their eggs warming in the flower beds. Who can live on that?

"You Never End with Hello"

> *Giving their eyes*
> *to summer*
> *their heads to the sky.*
>   —Pablo Neruda

Head in the stiff helmet, swathed in wet cotton, not quite dripping in my eyes.

How many turns of the pedals and the legs in a mile ride, a day's ride, a life?

According to Zeno, at any given moment I might as well be at rest. But I've never understood Zeno.

The wheels whirl, the road slides under, the planet spins, the whole system sails through space, a batch of flung gravel spiderwebbed by gravity.

Never mind. Stretch for the water bottle just in reach along the bottom bar, grab and squeeze, swirl and swallow, ice long gone but OK, squeeze and swallow, fit it back thinking again *this is the time I just fall over.*

Somebody ahead has a loud cold. Somebody whizzes past, two guys hunched into their high-dollar carbon fiber frames, talking too loud. Somebody loiters along with the kids, the boy wobbling wildly just for kicks.

Somebody has a command voice. Somebody is trying to explain. Someone has both feet locked in the pedals when the tire blows, like a gunshot, no warning.

The spare tube unreels like a weary snake, like a shed skin. The pump wheezes and complains. Somehow it works, well enough, for now.

The last miles are a slog and a sweat, but there is the last crossroads, there is the end of the way.

Tip off like cookies from a plate, softened by the sun. The next ride beckons, sweet and smooth. You never end with hello.

IV.

The boy who listened too hard

Late Explanation

I write out of indigestion, out of dejection, out of disdain and despair for the greed and venality of Those People.

You know who you are. OK, maybe I'm one too.

Because I want to think I'm trying.

Because I'm lazy, because I hate talking on the telephone, because I hate meetings even when I love the people in the meetings.

Because I don't want to explain.

Because so much needs to be explained.

Because some days I only want to heap up all my explanations and set them on fire.

Because I hope for smoke with the clean scent of maple and pine.

Because my parents let me play with matches, at least when it was time to burn trash in the barrel out back.

Because during the revival meetings we were not often threatened with fire but frequently reminded of hell.

Because I rarely burned anything I wasn't supposed to.

Because I had to put dead chickens in a wheelbarrow and throw them into the incinerator.

Because in summer after five or six days in the pit they'd fall right apart when I picked them up by the leg.

Because in my childhood this is what passed for trauma.

Because I did nothing to deserve my good fortune.

Because when the gas blazed up and caught their feathers and their flesh, the smoke flared up and out the chimney, and the harsh smell of burning replaced the brutal stink of decay, I could go in and wash for dinner.

Meditation with Gravel and Quilt

A powder clings to new gravel, a dust
of crushed rock that clings as well

to hands when you're moving it,
dropped from the heavy company

dump truck, so pushing at the pile
with the square-faced shovel you stumble,

break your fall as best you can, roll in shock
and inspect the damage, the white dust

and the blood welling through it, bits
of rock clinging, pale, not white but pale

against the roughened skin, against
the bright blood seeping, dripping,

and the aftershocks jangling through
your arms and legs, places that hurt

at once, those that hurt later, when
you've stumbled in to wash and whine

to your mother who frowns at first
but then fetches the washcloth

and the mercurochrome and a bandaid
or two, not to waste them where

there's just a scrape, where the air
will heal you fast as anything, where

the seeping won't stain her mother's quilt
when you slide under it hours from now,

the work day done and the fall
almost forgotten, the new rock

flattened with the tractor tires,
settling already into place.

Puff

I used to be a cloud
glum & silent & as high
as I could get above the dust
& gravel of the roads,
the muddy fields,
the corn harsh as hairbrushes.
Hot on the top
but cool underneath
I could survive I thought
if I kept sliding
on the moist currents,
if I kept all my secrets
& all my distance,
if I gave up forever
on the slender girls
in the next row,
the ones who seemed
wild and magical
as antelope or angels,
untouchable as stars.
I only dared glance
at them lest I vanish
in a puff of vapor
and young lust,
yes I was tempted
and afraid, yes
and stupid too,
we were all of us
not cloud or star
or angel but silly—
sweet & muddled-up
flesh & breath, yes,
& what a day when
someone turned & turned
her sweet warm face
to face me & yes
how my breath caught
when she did not
turn away.

Gundy Puzzles Over His Failure to Change His Name or Take Off to New York City to Become a Songwriter

> *"You're born, you know, the wrong names, wrong parents. I mean, that happens. You call yourself what you want to call yourself. This is the land of the free."*
> —Bob Dylan, 2004 interview

It never seemed to me I had
the wrong parents or the wrong name
though I did want different siblings at times
and to turn out of the lane onto the gravel
and just keep going . . . but no
who am I kidding
I went to the safe college
and the safe grad school and took
the first safe job offer and stayed
till I got another and settled
in the same gray house for decades
wearing small paths from home to office
office to home
only traveling gazillions of light years
in the pages of novels living various
other lives on planets & ships
& alien continents before retreating
to the same pretty good bed
plinking away at my big guitar
late at night now & then
nobody there to listen
the chords dying into whatever
new silence had been magicked into being
for nobody but me
whatever name I called myself
whatever I answered to
dancing on the windy beach
evening & sorrow & dawn
always almost a surprise
people still everywhere
for me to try to love
& some of them seem to love me

The Scale Model

I was bullied, and a bully myself, but I was also
almost the instrument being played. Main Street,

the window shades down, a friend was supposed
to visit but got lost in the cast-iron darkness

on the way into town. *Go cruelty free,* the model
citizens intoned. *We do not support culling of animals.*

But their bow ties and candy bars were useless
as petitions, as fake rose oil, as the ancient rituals

of ear candling and singing bowls. We can't
give away all our secrets, the commodore

confessed. *Jade* will rhyme with *raid* for
the foreseeable future. Those curls are gorgeous

but require extra care. Where will my love
of bird song, of cheesy puffs, of lemon zinger,

get me in the end? I could let the tincture steep
precisely long enough, loose, broad, fragrant,

and still find myself empty as the scale model,
clean and precise and ready to stand in anywhere.

The Professor Undertakes Metaphor

I believe I am a sheepdog,
yapping around
the edges of the flock,
eager to do my work,
to nip and harry
any foolish young lamb
back into the safety
of the herd,
the shelter of the fold,
to yap and badger,
keep a razor eye for wolves
and poachers, ravines
and swamps.
I want every lamb
to be safe.
I do not care
what they think.
I do not
give them choices.
I am not invested
in their feelings.
I do not listen unless
they stray or bleat in fear.
It is all for their own good.
I am really important.
I am very lonely.
I am so tired.

Soft Tissue

    (after "Good Bones," by Maggie Smith)

Pain is common, though we talk about it too little
or too much. Common as the tendons

in my rotator cuff—I strained or blew it out
trying not to fall on New Year's Eve, staying up

somehow, grateful but my right shoulder
screaming silently as I handed Joel the small things

I'd carried to his car, as I walked inside, my slippery
slippers gliding on snow. I know. It keeps me

up at night, makes me lie on the wrong side,
stabs at odd moments, but it's not so much.

For every bad shoulder there's a broken leg,
a cancer, six bad hearts, two thousand hands

and knees aching all day, all night. Once I asked
my class how many were hurting in their bodies,

right then, and all but three held up their hands.
I felt like a man who's lived his life in a soft cocoon,

oblivious, knees and hips and all the rest making
no great fuss while all around me friends and strangers

carried their secret aches and agonies, banked or blazing,
members of the secret club everybody has to join.

On the Condition of Rural America

1.
Oak pews hard as stone, plain walls, the clock ticking behind, where only the preacher could see. The preacher saying *Every head is bowed every eye is closed*, saying *Now is the time, if you feel God moving in your heart, if you are ready to surrender, if you are ready for His peace* . . . My eyes closed, my head bowed, awhirl, a hot stew of anxiety and confusion. What did I feel, what did I fear, what did I hear? If I raised my hand, if I walked to the front, what then? There would be questions, not unkind, but particular. What would I possibly say.

2.
I was more scared of going forward than ready for salvation, more frightened of the preacher's questions than of dying unsaved. And yet I was more scared of dying then, fifty years ago, than I am today. Kennedy was dead, Khrushchev was not. The missiles still trembled in their silos. The fields lay bare and black for months until the storms came, and then the snow blew like it meant to bury us all, ran for miles across the fields, assaulted the homesteads, an army with billions of tiny cold warriors. It piled between the buildings, blocked roads and driveways, white sand in all our gears.

3.
The schools and the churches were full then, but it took more and more acres to make a living, the tractors and the feedlots kept getting bigger, the farm kids had begun already to head off to the church colleges and the state schools, come out as doctors and sociologists, nurses and lawyers and business executives, instead of farm wives and farmers.

4.
Who wanted to be sitting in those hard pews at thirty, at sixty, at eighty, with the clock ticking down the seconds till your heart clutches and sighs and gives it up once for all? I wanted even then to keep my eyes open, to keep my head up. I wanted to look out of the pebbly windows, across the winter-bare plains, past the little huddled towns with their church spires and grain elevators, look out and to the long slow line of the horizon and the brilliant endless lens of the sky.

5.
But then it was autumn, and dark. My head was bowed, my eyes were closed. The preacher's voice was not harsh and not loud. He only asked that I fumble somehow into my deepest coverts, find and expose the soft creature there who had no desire to be examined or touched or interrogated, who wanted only to unfold like a night flower in its own time, to breathe quiet as grass in the dark, to find its way in solitude from what it was to something else.

The Smaller Mysteries on a Winter Sunday Morning

> *I become a transparent eye-ball. I am nothing; I see all . . . I am part or particle of God.*
> —Ralph Waldo Emerson, "Nature" (1849)
>
> *"Grand stand plays" are an abomination. Let the Gospel be presented in a plain, straightforward, and spirited manner.*
> —Daniel Kauffman, Manual of Bible Doctrines (1898)

Some people I've known for thirty years still seem like strangers.

Some people I've just met seem clear and close.

R. told me he's started putting a little dark sugar in his stir-fries, the day after mine turned out edible but a little drab.

When people become converted, said Daniel Kauffman, *their nature assumes a child-like simplicity.*

The student's father across the table yesterday, grease in the creases of his fingers and nails, too far away for me to ask what he does without feeling like a condescending fool.

The other father muttered to his son all through lunch, passing on things he'd gathered like a proud successful spy.

No M. in the choir today, she's off tending to her mother, who seems increasingly freed from this particular space and time.

G. sits downstairs now, with his mother who calls eight times a day, out of cookies or wondering where Darvin's been for so long.

H. is in hospice. J. is returning to PA without her husband and is grateful for our support.

I don't believe I've ever spoken to her.

The sermon title is "The Space Between Us." I'm in the balcony, not too close to anyone, though we're all in the same room.

The metaphor of society as a body was not favored by those eager to change the current order, the pastor says.

I think I'd rather be an eyeball than a toenail, a finger than a heel.

We don't have to become one big eye, the pastor says. *Communion is the resetting of the bones of the body of Christ.*

O Emerson, where art thou?

The most grievous [mistake] has been to mistake intelligence for spiritual power, wrote Daniel K.

I have my great-grandpa George's copy of his book.

He was a Mennonite preacher in the day when they didn't get paid, which Daniel K. says is as it should be. Maybe an offering twice a year.

His copy is little marked, but in the part on "Secret Societies" George underlined *Christ Himself testified, "In secret have I said nothing."*

My copy of Emerson is thatched with pencil lines. Transparent eyeballs, currents of the Universal Being. *In the woods there is perpetual youth. There is a crack in everything God has made.*

PONIES

> *When I'm the girl who daydreams her own funeral,*
> *then asks you about the salivary habit of ponies...*
> —Anna Journey

1.
I'm not a guy who gives much of a shit about ponies
or my funeral either. On the farm even my daydreams

were practical. Now when the snow falls I ponder
its capacity for paralysis, calculate its depth and which

shovel will annoy me least—usually the scoop shovel,
just like the ones we used to move shelled corn. I don't

start anything I can't finish in three days. OK, a week,
if drying time is involved. OK, except sabbaticals,

vacations, magazine subscriptions, gardens, a marriage,
and a bathroom project involving whole walls

of tile and endless grouting. It destroyed one entire
Christmas break but looks pretty good now.

2.
If there's shit under my fingernails it's surely
my own. This has not always been true.

I did my modern father duty, wiped plenty of butts
and rinsed countless diapers and only lost two

down the toilet. I know the ammoniac stench
of a heavy diaper pail poured into the washer,

the suspense about it splashing over, the relief
as the lid comes down.

3.
So forgive me, please, if I've spent too long reckoning
my own numbers. I scan the obituaries now,

looking only at the dates. I walk like a penguin
when the snow falls. I know the trickiest day comes later,

after traffic and footsteps, after the melts and freezes,
when we all tire of taking care. Somebody will take

a bad fall. The headache will ease and then get worse,
the fluids seep in, the pressure escalate. I *do* want a pony.

Some Sentences for a Man Who Won't Read Them

He was the star running back of the first great football team at Flanagan High, not long after the Last Good War.

When I was in high school his name was still on the record board for the 440—54.1.

Now he has a four-pointed cane, and one shoe with a brace that wraps his calf.

He always said his brother Jim had run 52.9 a year or two later.

Now he asks what the plan is, and asks again in twenty minutes.

He and Mom were king and queen of the first homecoming. They didn't dance, but already they were sweethearts.

Now Mom reminds him to use the back bathroom, and sometimes he remembers.

He taught me to throw and to catch, to buckle down, to carry two buckets of water for balance, to turn back and look for the buttonweeds we'd missed.

He planted straight rows for fifty years, got up early, worked till dark, napped in his chair when he could.

He and Mom put six of us through college, tended thousands of chickens, gathered millions of eggs.

When they moved to town he still drove out every day to help Gary, ran the combine and the big tractors, hauled grain to town, cleaned and greased the tractors and implements, sorted tools and seed.

A couple of years ago Gary started to tell us about little accidents. Dad caught a bin with the end of the field cultivator, punched a hole in it. He never quite got the six steps to start the newest tractor straight in his head.

With him I put a new roof on our first garage, sad and rickety as it was.

We stretched new carpet in the tiny house, scraped, painted. Mom was better help with the wallpaper, but he was good at everything else.

We traded off driving the run-down U-Haul all the way from Kansas to Bluffton,

Gary and Mom and Marlyce and the kids behind us in the station wagon.

We hauled our secondhand furniture, plates and clothes into our new old house, made a long row of cardboard boxes by the street.

It poured the next morning, and they sagged in the rain like the saddest, smallest, oldest mountains ever.

Nice People

> *Writers aren't people exactly.*
> —F. Scott Fitzgerald
> *There was a band playin in my head . . .*
> —Neil Young

Yesterday a guy who knows Richie Furay,
late of Buffalo Springfield, let the whole internet
or at least my Facebook page know that
by his lights Neil Young is not that nice a person,
and that furthermore Richie Furay is indeed
a nice person. I've never been in a room
with Richie Furay or Neil Young. I don't really
doubt that Neil Young was mean and wrong
half a century ago when he blew off Richie Furay
and Buffalo Springfield. But I know for sure that
Richie Furay didn't change my life and Neil Young
did, singing in that high whine that should have
been pure annoyance but somehow wasn't,
playing guitar solos that stayed on the same note
longer than anybody else would have dared,
out of sheer nerve, ego, boredom, rage
or God knows what, solos I haven't heard
in years but still know by heart, songs about
heartbreak and disaster. *Down by the river,
I shot my baby.* Who the hell would do that?
Not Neil Young, surely. The song is not clear,
and more clarity would not improve it. Writers.
*Or, if they're any good, they're a whole lot of people
trying so hard to be one person,* said Fitzgerald,
who knew all about trying so hard. *I am a parcel
of vain strivings tied / By a chance bond together,*
wrote that poser Thoreau, chasing a loon
around the pond, never getting close enough
to please himself, but close enough to write
about it. Writers aren't people exactly,
let alone nice people. Guitars in need
of someone to play them and a big Fender
amp, or rock bands that broke up decades ago,
or channels for this voice, that voice. Listeners.
The banks of the river. Not the river.

Tablets

All I ever wanted was to walk at the head of this strong new tribe, to have everyone hush when I say to them, *hush*, to choose from all the wide forking paths which path we should take among the lilacs, the dogwoods, the maples and the violets and the birdsong, to hear the whisper of sandals in the new grass behind me and begin to wonder who is cold and who is tired, who is bored and getting sulky.

But to come safe to the windy table and ask everyone to sit and to bend to their tablets as if to plates of meat and bread. To hold my tablet open in the raw wind and wish for calm, for sun, know that soon I must rise and break silence as though it is mine to keep or destroy, as though what I think is what matters,

as though the trust of these children no longer children is something I deserve when I am the one who has brought them into the windy spring with no reasons or excuses, with nothing to eat and no fire to make, when Katie has pulled up her socks and Christina still has the violet between her teeth and Brett is still looking and writing though his arms are blue.

I wish I could stand like a tree and warm them but no, what will I do next, what now, I can wish if I want for less wind and more sun, I can listen as they speak their new words and say *yes, yes,* and say *now we can go* and rise with the rest and return to the warm room in the midst of my beautiful, temporary tribe.

Life in the Complex

> *You are perfectly safe while you wait.*
> *There is plenty of air and the elevator cannot fall.*
> —Note above elevator control panel

—In memoriam, Rudy and Irene Martens

There is plenty of safety and a lock on every door.

The young men on the sidewalk do not notice you,
even if you slip onto the balcony to rearrange
the plastic flowers. They yell, but not at you.

The patterns on the chairs are good for a hundred years.
The coffee maker shut off on its own
seven weeks and two hours ago.

The portraits of Pinkie and Blue Boy gaze out,
blank and imperious, and whenever you notice
you think of your daughter painting them by number
and how bored she must have been that summer.

When sleep won't come there's the TV
and the tinny voices that speak
of things as they are or should be
for as long as you need them, never ask
the wrong questions, offer their endless
skeins of words that hold you like
the elevator cables hidden out of sight,
words you breathe like the plentiful air.

You are perfectly safe while you wait.

How We Learned to Love Our Bodies

We saved ourselves for the wedding night
but decided quickly that was a big mistake,

whole Saharas of lost time. But never mind.
It was like falling into the Grand Canyon

in fine new android bodies, then kicking on
the jets and launching ourselves upward

until the sky turned black. Breathing?
Who needs air when you've got stars

like blazing sand, when the moon is gaudy
as any shameless dancer's breast? (Pages

and reams of intricate data, suppressed.)
Nobody saw us land. Nobody on the streets.

Nobody in the shops. At last we lay down
weary and happy in a broken-down storeroom,

and slipped into sleep and woke up back on earth.

Lessons of a Gentle Childhood

Under this skylight many lost things are visible.
I see the mighty black and yellow spiders in the iris beds

by the old garage, and feel not a shred of fear.
I could husk two dozen sticky ears of sweet corn

and pick two quarts of strawberries on my achy knees
without whining once. I could hit four baseballs

in a row under the maple trees and over the fence,
the only kind of home run that counts in my private game.

I could sit through the whole Sunday night service
in the stickiest dusk of July and not once imagine

committing the unpardonable sin, just to see
if anything would change. I could sing *Just as I am,*

thine own to be seven times through and never switch
to "Mr. Tambourine Man" in my head, never dream

of dancing neath the diamond sky, just as I am
thine own to be, silhouetted by the sea, without

a single plea, hey, hey, I am weary, play another song
for me, an old song that I've never heard, play it

smooth and loud and long, play "The Boy Who Listened
Too Hard," play "The Boy with Dirt in His Nose."

Play "The Boy with the Lousy Guitar in His Arms,"
play "The Boy Whose Eyes Are Still Closed."

About the Author

Jeff Gundy's seventh book of poems, *Abandoned Homeland* (Bottom Dog Press, 2015) was a finalist for the Ohioana Poetry Award, and he was named Ohio Poet of the Year for *Somewhere Near Defiance* (Anhinga, 2014). His earlier books with Bottom Dog Press include *Rhapsody with Dark Matter* (2002) and *Inquiries* (1992). *Songs from an Empty Cage: Poetry, Mystery, Anabaptism, and Peace* (Cascadia, 2013), and *Walker in the Fog: On Mennonite Writing* (Cascadia, 2005), winner of the Dale Brown award, are the most recent of his four prose books. His poems and essays have appeared in *The Georgia Review*, *The Sun*, *Kenyon Review*, *Crazyhorse*, *Christian Century*, *Image*, and many other journals. Other grants and lectureships include multiple Ohio Arts Council grants and Pushcart nominations and two C. Henry Smith Peace Lectureships.

Gundy is professor of English at Bluffton University in Ohio and director of the Bluffton University Research Center, and spent his last two sabbaticals teaching at LCC International University in Klaipeda, Lithuania (2015) and as a Fulbright lecturer and poet in residence at the University of Salzburg, Austria (2008). He and his wife Marlyce have three grown sons, five grandchildren, four granddogs, and have logged several thousand miles on their bright yellow Cannondale tandem.

Acknowledgements Continued

Christian Century: "Contemplation with Red Bridge and Windy Sunshine," "On the Way to Denver," "Cold Day in the Provinces," "Determinism on a Summer Morning in the Midwest"
Forklift, Ohio: "Nice People"
The Georgia Review: "God Is Not Right, He Is Big," "Notes toward Intuitive Geography"
Image: "Theodicy with Tents and Masonry," "Lessons of a Gentle Childhood"
Journal of Mennonite Studies: "The Smaller Mysteries on a Winter Sunday Morning"
Lake Effect: "Nothing Is Level There," "Soft Tissue"
Nimrod: "Meditation on Solitude and Simplicity"
The Other Journal: "On the Condition of Rural America," "September: 9 Variations"
Poetry Salzburg Review: "Speaking Truth in the Most Human Way"
Resist Much Obey Little: Inaugural Poems to the Resistance: "Think Like a Tree"
Saint Katherine Review: "Magpie on Highway 221," "Late Explanation"
Shalith: "Puff"
Slippery Elm: "Things Overheard, Observed, and Possibly Misunderstood"
Terrain: "Meditation with Salal and Otters," "Uneasy Fantasia from Quarry Hollow," "Traces"
Topology: "The God of Dirt," "Spring Ode with Robins and Mallards"
"Plain Advice" was reprinted by the Academy of American Poets at poets.org.

Books by Bottom Dog Press
Appalachian Writing Series

Old Brown, by Craig Paulenich, 92 pgs, $16
A Wounded Snake: A Novel, by Joseph G. Anthony, 262 pgs, $18
Brown Bottle: A Novel, by Sheldon Lee Compton, 162 pgs, $18
A Small Room with Trouble on My Mind, by Michael Henson, 164 pgs, $18
Drone String: Poems, by Sherry Cook Stanforth, 92 pgs, $16
Voices from the Appalachian Coalfields, by Mike and Ruth Yarrow,
Photos by Douglas Yarrow, 152 pgs, $17
Wanted: Good Family, by Joseph G. Anthony, 212 pgs, $18
Sky Under the Roof: Poems, by Hilda Downer, 126 pgs, $16
Green-Silver and Silent: Poems, by Marc Harshman, 90 pgs, $16
The Homegoing: A Novel, by Michael Olin-Hitt, 180 pgs, $18
She Who Is Like a Mare: Poems of Mary Breckinridge and the Frontier Nursing Service,
by Karen Kotrba, 96 pgs, $16
Smoke: Poems, by Jeanne Bryner, 96 pgs, $16
Broken Collar: A Novel, by Ron Mitchell, 234 pgs, $18
The Pattern Maker's Daughter: Poems, by Sandee Gertz Umbach, 90 pgs, $16
The Free Farm: A Novel, by Larry Smith, 306 pgs, $18
Sinners of Sanction County: Stories, by Charles Dodd White, 160 pgs, $17
Learning How: Stories, Yarns & Tales, by Richard Hague, $18
The Long River Home: A Novel, by Larry Smith, 230 pgs, cloth $22; paper $16
Eclipse: Stories, by Jeanne Bryner, 150 pgs, $16

Appalachian Writing Series Anthologies

Unbroken Circle: Stories of Cultural Diversity in the South,
Eds. Julia Watts and Larry Smith, 194 pgs, $17
Appalachia Now: Short Stories of Contemporary Appalachia,
Eds. Charles Dodd White and Larry Smith, 178 pgs, $17
Degrees of Elevation: Short Stories of Contemporary Appalachia,
Eds. Charles Dodd White and Page Seay, 186 pgs, $16

BOOKS BY BOTTOM DOG PRESS
HARMONY SERIES

Without a Plea, by Jeff Gundy, 96 pgs, $16
Taking a Walk in My Animal Hat, by Charlene Fix, 90 pgs, $16
Earnest Occupations, by Richard Hague, 200 pgs, $18
Pieces: A Composite Novel, by Mary Ann McGuigan, 250 pgs, $18
Crows in the Jukebox: Poems, by Mike James, 106 pgs, $16
Portrait of the Artist as a Bingo Worker: A Memoir, by Lori Jakiela, 216 pgs, $18
The Thick of Thin: A Memoir, by Larry Smith, 238 pgs, $18
Cold Air Return: A Novel, by Patrick Lawrence O'Keeffe, 390 pgs, $20
Flesh and Stones: A Memoir, by Jan Shoemaker, 176 pgs, $18
Waiting to Begin: A Memoir, by Patricia O'Donnell, 166 pgs, $18
And Waking: Poems, by Kevin Casey, 80 pgs, $16
Both Shoes Off: Poems, by Jeanne Bryner, 112 pgs, $16
Abandoned Homeland: Poems, by Jeff Gundy, 96 pgs, $16
Stolen Child: A Novel, by Suzanne Kelly, 338 pgs, $18
The Canary: A Novel, by Michael Loyd Gray, 196 pgs, $18
On the Flyleaf: Poems, by Herbert Woodward Martin, 106 pgs, $16
The Harmonist at Nightfall: Poems of Indiana, by Shari Wagner, 114 pgs, $16
Painting Bridges: A Novel, by Patricia Averbach, 234 pgs, $18
Ariadne & Other Poems, by Ingrid Swanberg, 120 pgs, $16
The Search for the Reason Why: New and Selected Poems, by Tom Kryss,
192 pgs, $16
Kenneth Patchen: Rebel Poet in America, by Larry Smith,
Revised 2nd Edition, 326 pgs, Cloth $28
Selected Correspondence of Kenneth Patchen,
Edited with introduction by Allen Frost, Paper $18/ Cloth $28
Awash with Roses: Collected Love Poems of Kenneth Patchen,
Eds. Laura Smith and Larry Smith with introduction by Larry Smith, 200 pgs, $16
Breathing the West: Great Basin Poems, by Liane Ellison Norman, 96 pgs, $16
Maggot: A Novel, by Robert Flanagan, 262 pgs, $18
American Poet: A Novel, by Jeff Vande Zande, 200 pgs, $18
The Way-Back Room: Memoir of a Detroit Childhood, by Mary Minock, 216 pgs, $18

BOTTOM DOG PRESS, INC.

P.O. BOX 425 /HURON, OHIO 44839
HTTP://SMITHDOCS.NET

www.ingramcontent.com/pod-product-compliance
Lightning Source LLC
Chambersburg PA
CBHW021021090426
42738CB00007B/857